EMPORIUM

IAN PINDAR was born in London in 1970. He is the author of *Joyce* (Haus, 2004), a biography of James Joyce, and co-translated *The Three Ecologies* (Continuum, 2000) by the radical French theorist Félix Guattari. He was an editor at J. M. Dent, Weidenfeld & Nicolson and the Harvill Press, where he edited works by Haruki Murakami, Anna Politkovskaya and W. G. Sebald. He is now a freelance writer and editor, and regularly contributes to the *Guardian* and the *Times Literary Supplement*. He won second prize in the 2009 National Poetry Competition, was shortlisted for the 2010 Forward Prize (Best Single Poem), won a runners-up prize in the Bridport Prize 2010, and is the recipient of an award from the Arthur Welton Foundation. He lives in Oxfordshire.

T0290278

IAN PINDAR

Emporium

CARCANET

First published in Great Britain in 2011 by

Carcanet Press Limited
Alliance House
Cross Street
Manchester M2 7AQ

A CIP catalogue record for this book is available from the British Library

ISBN 978 1 84777 065 3

The publisher acknowledges financial assistance from Arts Council England

Typeset by XL Publishing Services, Tiverton
Printed and bound in England by SRP Ltd, Exeter

for Ali

My awful seventies
name, you sd
(mine too) but
no

From alle wimmen my love is lent,
And light on Alisoun

Anonymous
circa 1300

Levedy, al for thine sake

Armed with certain relics, I began to assemble an emporium where nothing in it would be for sale – a shop that would never open.

MALCOLM MCLAREN

ACKNOWLEDGEMENTS

The author gratefully acknowledges the following publications in which poems in *Emporium* first appeared, sometimes in slightly different form: *The London Magazine*, *Magma*, *New Poetries III* (Carcanet Press), *Oxford Poetry*, *PN Review*, *Poetry Review*, *Stand* and the *Times Literary Supplement*. Thanks are also due to Michael Schmidt, Judith Willson and all at Carcanet for their support. Invaluable advice was offered by John Crowfoot regarding 'Birds', and Dana Pšenicová at the Czech Embassy in London helped me with 'Mrs Beltinska in the Bath', which won second prize in the 2009 National Poetry Competition and was shortlisted for the 2010 Forward Prize (Best Single Poem).

CONTENTS

Emporium

FIGURE STUDY

Naked on a bed, the sex in shadow,
not caring if man or woman.

Something of the caged beast, captive, fallow,
odour of unclean linen.

Darkness beyond everything.
Nothing visible except

limbs turning, seeking rest,
arms and legs bending, unbending

like a puppet examining its joints.
The head moving from side to side

as if struck by invisible fists
from different angles, from inside.

MRS BELTINSKA IN THE BATH

Pavel in profile
his eye at the spyhole
watches Mrs Beltinska in the bath.

Steam from the spyhole
rises and unravels in the dark
cold apartment at his back,

where a TV with the sound down
shows the River Vltava
bursting its banks.

And as Prague's metro floods
and the Malá Strana floods
and the Waldstein Palace floods

and the National Theatre floods
and the Kampa Modern Art Museum floods,
Mrs Beltinska sinks her treasures in the suds.

The first Czech bible (1488) is drowned
in sewage water, but the warm orange glow
from Mrs Beltinska's bathroom

coming through the spyhole
gives an odd kind of halo
to Pavel's head seen from behind.

ON THE FRENCH RIVIERA

Youth and beauty have left me
  a full packet of cigarettes
and this balcony. Time redecorates
  my home as a reliquary.

The camera loved me once,
  as everyone loves a young woman
of spirit who toys with men
  and uses her natural elegance

to get what she wants. Siren
  or ingénue, whatever they asked of me
I exuded 'a carefree, naive sexuality',
  the critics said. Dominique, is that Dorian

at the door? My official biographer
  promised to swing by after church
with more questions. He isn't much
  to look at, but he's my last admirer.

MONSTERS OF PHILOSOPHY

There are monsters on the prowl whose form changes
with the history of knowledge.
MICHEL FOUCAULT

Scepticism is insincere
   If not maintained in daily life,
Professor Aromax concludes
   While murdering his second wife.

Ideas, we are told by James,
   Are true if they are profitable.
Professor Bidex keeps a shrunken
   Head upon her coffee table.

Professor MacIntyre expounds
   At length upon his idées fixes,
But hastily departs if any
   Student wears a crucifix.

Professor Pyke is much the same
   And has no tolerance for God.
His last dispute resulted in
   A bloody carcass in the quad.

The students of Professor Stead
   Know better than to mock his stammer.
The last to do so had his head
   Caved in by someone with a hammer.

Professor Mallard has a coat
   Of thick and matted body hair,
But only when the moon is full,
   At other times it isn't there.

Professor Gant, a revenant,
  Who rarely ever takes the stairs,
Prefers to glide from room to room,
  Catching students unawares.

And still the ghost of Francis Bacon
  Haunts the winding stair below,
Doomed for a certain term to stuff
  A chicken carcass full of snow.

A DOG ONE AFTERNOON

I

In a nearby exhibition hall
Mr Ponsonby-Smythe demonstrates his new machine
for winning back the Empire – there is blood
    all over his doeskin pantaloons.

In a pagoda surrounded by bamboo
Miss Grace Laluah serves coconut milk,
    bananas with honey and tropical fruits . . .

But who is that girl in the wicker chair,
her arm amputated at the elbow?
    Her copper hair and small breasts delight me:
the standard lamp, the single bed, the curtained window.
    She looks
                sad
                anaemic
                telegenic.

Her skin smells of pepper.

II

        Alienated again.
        In the doghouse.
        I am a dog and I don't even like dogs
        (I'm a dog and I don't even like them).
Skulking through the streets like a dog.
Licking old wounds like a dog.

        Something's missing.
        Have you forgotten
        anything?

None of this was made for your
        entertainment.

        (So tired, so tired.
        Work tomorrow . . .)

First there was sleep, then waking
        then making do, then sleep.

        And when night falls
        and the will fails,
        when the will fails
        and night falls,
        all the poisons within me,
all the poisons in which I am mired
        accumulate in the marrow.

SOCIETY OF BLOOD

They will be smiling as they did of old,
keeping tradition in the blood
and blood in the soil.

      Men of action, irrational,
suspicious of intellect: all dissent
is betrayal and betrayal death.

      Fear difference: the enemy
within. If you are weak
you will die, as Nature intended.

      And the people perish,
reeling, staggering towards
a ring of light on the horizon.

ANECDOTE OF THE CAR

I drove a car to Chambourcy
And left it there, without a thought.
It hurt the owner of that car
To think of it.

The kindly Camboriciens
Prayed for its soul at St Clothilde.
The car was bound to play them false
It was a wicked, wilful car.

Its classic parts, so very rare,
Were polished there with tender care.
Its engine all of burnished gold
It did not care for man or God.

MARC CHAGALL
THE POET RECLINING

Time was when the poet lay in a green field.

Ezra Pound

O I once met a poet reclining
For a pillow he had but a coat
And I saw his green halo a-shining
Green halo, green halo, he wrote.

> *Green halo*
> *Green halo*

Alone at last in the country
With a pig and a horse in a field
With pine trees and woods all around me
My heart at last shall be healed.

> *Green halo*
> *Green halo*

Now I have no farmer's wisdom
And grow here nary a bean
But the woodland makes me welcome
And the grass my halo green.

> *Green halo*
> *Green halo*

PARABLE

I

Here they come, judging
my parable,
the one about the highway and
the blackbird

The distance
between them
always already
expanding.

II

(You can see the whole thing as
a ceaseless, dynamic
movement.)

III

It is not solitude or the last
physical delight that
troubles you but night and its quick
arrows – the
fearful, the
threatened, the
miserable – but
you are your own
purpose,
at ease with a life
incomparable.

IV

(So much leads to thinking otherwise.)

V

The rubble of sundown is
more than a way of commenting on
      the disease
    of civilisation.

          In those long
shadows I lost my voice. I
lost the argument. My fingers slipped
You lowered   so that

The touch was

          and it excited us

VI

Rooms and passageways.
We need to find some-
where they cannot search –

the provocation of
a fire escape takes us
down
across town and
away from the losses of the day

the loosened thought of heat and
nothing to say.

ADVICE FOR TRAVELLERS

So she was left to dissolve under a starless
heaven, reduced by perspective to something like
      a stick,
no ordinary suffering.

The machinery of mud is good at living
with dead things. Bog angel with borrowed teeth and stones
      for eyes,
which close and listen for a voice

that doesn't cry out. I don't know how she got there.
Did she even visit the nearby city,
      each street
arranged according to the movements

of celestial bodies, where twin pyramids
keep twin volcanoes company? The sun rises
      every day
behind the temple, rain falls on

the ancient mud gods and the locals hunt or make
fire or love, depending on their fancy. It's a
      great place
to shop for traditional items –

necklaces of human teeth, the sacrificial
harvest – and it's fun to people-watch. Those people,
      for instance,
being led in procession:
      at noon
their blood will run in the streets.

POEM

When one god
claimed to be

the only god

the other gods died

laughing

WHAT IS THE MATTER?

What is the
matter?

To speak of
matter

To speak in
matter

matter-word
word-matter

in matter
matter speaks
the Word

ARCHAEOLOGIES

Shell holes and standing water
    Brown metal open to
    the elements
Empty barrels   broken pails
Corrugated iron   weeds and silence

The silhouette of a man
hangs from a telegraph pole against a sky
  the colour of bile

Silent electric wires lead
  nowhere
  and in the distance
Rusted armaments   puddles
Train tracks

Mud sucks on raw heels

The distant waterfall calls us

The constant sound of running water
      drips
      echoes
Everything sweats
    with moisture

In a clear stream
  a pocket watch among pebbles . . .

'Hey you, do you know where we are?'

Warming ourselves by this brazier
Rolling cigarettes under the ruins   drinking
      rosehip brandy
Gold has no meaning any more than
Charity

We don't drink
the water

Goldenhair crawling with lice

This leech on the back of my hand
woke me   I need a piss

A woman cries out in the night . . .

'Hey you, do you know where we are?'

White stones worn smooth
Smooth humps of vegetable matter
steaming from afar

Weak sun of celebration
Late flowers among nettles
Pulling potatoes out of the peat

Salted herring at noon
This awful coffee

Yesterday the heat
The light receded   the shadows tapered into long rays . . .

'Hey you, do you know where we are?'

How comforting a light in the darkness
Any light

Every fire is a woman – remembered desire

We got the headlights working again but
Nothing else   then the headlights died . . .

At dawn above the trees a
Helicopter
Doesn't land

Nor do we hail it
Not knowing
Where we stand

SNOW

on a metal contraption of some kind
erected in the woods, the height of a man,

can be knocked off with a black branch,
revealing tiny rivets, a bolt or two,

but nothing more of the machine's purpose
than can be guessed at from its peculiar shape

and solitary position
out here where nobody lives or works or ever comes

with only the wolves for company,
howling in the wind that whistles through its delicate wires
    sending us to sleep.

THE KING'S EVIL

There are no kings inside the Gates of Eden
BOB DYLAN

A pox on all kings!
AN OLD WOMAN, WATCHING CHARLES II'S
ENTRY INTO LONDON, 1660

And it isn't a question of money –
how much the monarchy costs –
but they set up a right by assumption,
by assumption binding posterity

    And Thomas Paine began
    the *Rights of Man*
    in a room above
    The Angel Inn, Islington,
    attacking the very basis
    of slavery
    arguing that we are all born free

    free and equal in rights
    and have a natural right
    to free speech, freedom of conscience,
    life and liberty

Yet we are subject to one family:
the monarch
and close relatives of the monarch
and the monarch is first and foremost political

    They sought to suppress
    the *Rights of Man*
    and indicted Paine
    for seditious libel
    and Paine fled to France
    and was tried *in absentia*
    and the jury was offered
    two guineas and dinner to find him guilty

and the bookseller Thomas Spence
imprisoned for selling the *Rights of Man*

America threw off the yoke
of monarchy. France threw off the yoke
of monarchy. But we are ruled over
in perpetuity
by one family
and this is regarded as normal
in a democracy
bloodlines and blood fascism
in a democracy
destiny written in our veins

'we high-born ones', 'we well-bred
with pure blood and pure breeding'
– 'our superior genetics'[1] –
born to rule
to master
No rational basis but blood
(and some idiot always says:
'They know how to rule –
it's in their blood')

But Paine was clear on this:
hereditary rule
precludes the consent
of succeeding generations
and the *preclusion of consent* is
DESPOTISM

And the monarch will make retribution
the Tower of London
once a place of execution
and on Tower Bridge strange to see
the hair of the head disappear
the gristle of the nose consumed away
the eye sockets . . .

1 'I was brought up to do this sort of work. It is training, experience and genetics.'
Prince Andrew, HRH the Duke of York (*Telegraph*, 24.10.09).

                    All deference is fear
and not meeting the monarch's eyes
          is fear and servile fearfulness:
'To monarchize,
          be fear'd and kill with looks . . . '

And the monarch is above the law
          Crown Immunity
and the Privy Council shrouded in mystery
and the keeper of the monarchy the BBC
and every royal wedding is a funeral
          for democracy;
and our elected representatives reprimanded
for mentioning the monarch in the House
and the misinformed multitude
          wave flags and worship
          wave flags and worship
a phantom at the rotten core
          of our botched democracy.

LES VACANCES DE MONSIEUR P.

P. lay in a narrow cot in what one might call
A state of profound erotic affection
For *La Belle France* and all things French. The only work
He had to do that day was to say
In a postcard that he was enjoying his holiday,
Then relax and spend the remainder

Of his time resting. He was eating the remainder
Of some kind of pastry – but what to call
It? Why bother with words? He was on holiday!
And he believed it made him an object of affection
Not to speak French, but to point and say
Nothing. Learning a language is hard work.

He was English, which everyone seemed to work
Out from his appearance, some remainder
Of home. In his postcard he did not say
He had been kept awake by the mating call
Of an Australian, screwing the object of his affection
Into a wall. For Australian backpackers also holiday

In Paris in November, when it's cheap. I could have a holiday
Romance, thought P., but would it work?
Could incomprehension increase affection?
We might happily spend the remainder
Of our lives in silence, but could one call
It love without language? Who could say?

P. realised he had a lot that he wanted to say
To a girl in England and he spent his holiday
Pestering her with call after call after call . . .
Some days he couldn't get the public telephone to work,
Others she was not at liberty to talk. For the remainder
He spoke openly, declaring his affection.

He knew little about love, but sensed this affection
Might not be shared when he heard her say,
'You don't have to call me every day.' He was deaf to the remainder
Of their conversation. P. would try to enjoy his holiday,
Although from that moment on he had his work
Cut out. For even P. couldn't call

This love or even affection. And that one phone call
Ruined the remainder of what he laughably called his holiday.
But that isn't to say he was glad to get back to work.

CHAIN LETTER

Fastyng on a Friday forth gan he wende
Unto the bed wher that sche slepte,
And she was cleped madame Eglentyne,
Besely seking with a continuell chaunge
To change her hew, and sundry formes to don,
Studying inventions fine, her wits to entertaine:
With sweet musk-roses and with eglantine.
(He is starke mad, who ever sayes
Ill matching words and deeds long past or late
Could by industrious Valour climbe
Above the rest, their discords to decide.)
Proceeding on, the lovely Goddess
Asleep and naked as an Indian lay,
Of such, as wand'ring near her secret bow'r,
By youthful heat and female art
Of varied beauty, to delight the wanderer and repose
Wi' favours, secret, sweet, and precious.
His look and bending figure, all bespeak
A stifled, drowsy, unimpassion'd grief,
That he was forced, against his will, no doubt,
To own that death itself must be
Where there is neither sense of life or joys.
Anxious her lips, her breathing quick and short:
Her eyes blazed upon him – 'And *you!* You bring us your vices
so near
And this gray spirit yearning in desire
As if alive. Will't please you rise? We'll meet
And hand in hand, on the edge of the sand,
Stepping with light feet . . . swiftly and noiselessly stepping and
stopping
Where the sea meets the moon-blanch'd land,
The sighing sound, the lights around the shore,
The irresponsive sounding of the sea,
Untouched by morning and untouched by noon,
We can begin to feed.
Let us go hence together without fear.
I see what you are doing: you are leading me on.

What hours, O what black hoürs we have spent.
Some love too little, some too long,
Though both are foolish, both are strong
An' they talks a lot o' lovin', but wot do they understand?
Consume my heart away; sick with desire,
I forgive you everything and there is nothing to forgive.
Now the mind lays by its trouble and considers
Openair love and religion's reform,
The riddle of a man and a woman
All heavy with sleep, fucked girls and fat leopards.
Queer, what a dim dark smudge you have disappeared into!
Drifted away . . . O, but Everyone
is an enchanted thing
A pulse in the eternal mind, no less.
The songsters of the air repair
The hopelessness. Whatever hope is yours
Humanity i love you
and I am glad that you do not belong
Under a world of whistles, wire and steam.
A city seems between us. It is only love.
I take my curses back.
Only sometimes when a tree has fallen
In splendor and dissipation
In a world of sunlight where nothing is amiss
I feel as though I had begun to fall,
the whole misery diagnosed undiagnosed misdiagnosed.
Think of what our Nation stands for
Of Captain Ferguson
In silk hat. Daylight.
The light is in the east. Yes. And we must rise, act. Yet
He didn't fight.
he played dominoes and drank calvados unTil
They put him in the fields to dock swedes,
And the craters of his eyes grew springshoots and fire
And forty-seven years went by like Einstein.
My mind's not right.
I too have ridden boxcars boxcars boxcars.'
(An ode? Pindar's art, the editors tell us, was not a statue but a
source for bugling echoes and silvered laments. The
Power of some sort or other will go on

In the network, in the ruin.
We repeat our conversation in the glittering dark.
One – someone – stops to break off a bit of myrtle and recite all
                                                    the lines.)

If woman is inconstant,
How I loved those made of stone. And yet poetry has
Tough lips that cannot quite make the sounds of love,
strange hairy lips behind
and I am sweating a lot by now and thinking of
long legs, long waist, high breasts (no bra), long
confessions. Lady, I follow.
And still the machinery of the great exegesis is only beginning,
it will Invent a whole new literachure
From a cacophony of dusty forms . . .
O but what about love? I forget love.
The sun dries me as I dance
On the flowers of Eden.
Platonic England, house of solitudes,
I have hung our cave with roses.
O the dark caves of obligation.
I remember when I lived in Boston reading all of Dostoyevsky's
                                    novels one right after the other
And yet last night I played *Meditations*,
fugitive dialogue of masterwork.
Perhaps I've got to write better longer thinking of it as
echo-soundings, searches, probes, allurements.
A few months earlier I had taken a creative writing class:
'The period in history termed Modern is now over' it said.
Suddenly I feel silly and ill. This apartment
invents the world, holds it together in color of
your body waking up so sweet to me   skin
we sit on the bed Indian fashion not touching . . .
I was working on a different poem.
It was words that detained us, though they do not reach
the crush of it, the variety,
in which history itself is vanquished,
When he names the forgotten names
as if they might start speaking.

OF TRUTH

There was such a truth once.
I remember it. We all shared it
like a candle in the dark.

During the war a piece of bone
got lodged in it, but you
didn't hear it complaining.

In a cinema after the war
I saw it looking for its hat
under the seats.
It was smaller then, a little hunched.

I don't recall the last time
we met. I think it was in Berlin.
I'd just been to the lavatory
when I came out
to find a girl in blue jeans
staring at a patch of oil in the corridor.

Something moved in the darkness
and I stamped on it.

SUGGESTIONS FOR FURTHER READING

When Gypsies first appeared in Europe
ordinary people began to sit

on chairs and hallmarks were
required for silver objects. I intended to go

to Geneva to fetch my wife, but then
playing cards became popular,

and opera and privacy were
invented, as well as the

mechanical clock. Midnight struck
in a domestic interior.

TWO FIGS

Upstairs two of them were
posing in states of rhapsodic
abandon, their skin rough and
blemished, not like

those good-looking girls, genteel
sisters, standing against
Chinese tapestries in
Vienna. They squeeze

the hearts of men, are
sardonic, flippant and intense and
for their heads the season weaves
spring flowers

into a crown. A greyhound,
a mandolin, a fruit dish with
pears, two figs
on a table.

THE PROPHECIES

I

When Venus is covered by the sun
a broken nose will break its heart
and a question mark will hover over
a futon in Finsbury Park.

In February a man named Pixon or Pixer
will grow a beard in a disputed region.
Conversations will be interrupted, disconnected,
leading to the degeneration of knowledge.

A vixen will be lost in Leicester Square
and two peacocks will suffer paroxysms
in Hyde Park, near a cinema complex.

A woman with small feet will eat
salted squid in Chinatown
and strawberries, a prelude to sex.

II

In June the instincts will go
backwards, dragging the economy. Riches
will turn to rags and winos will be sober, ushering in
an era of Total Responsibility.

A man who fears his madness but rebels
against psychoanalysis
will leave his umbrella behind
in an area known as Luxor.

Late summer will bear witness to the erection of
stone fences, howls and ghastly cries near
London, New York, Paris.

Oh what abominable executions will occur
before the planets realign, and a boy shot and killed
in Colorado will be found working in a pizza parlour.

CASANOVA

He is unique, like everyone else.
There is no second chance, no afterlife.

All he wants is to be a real Casanova,
give his partner complete satisfaction,

clear his existing credit,
amaze his friends with his feats of memory,

save money on a lawnmower.
He can go neither forwards nor back.

They mock his accent, astonish him with their predictions.
He tries to kill his adopted son.

The walls of the room fall away to reveal
a cement horizon. He waits for his connection.

CĀRVĀKA/LOKĀYATA

Many wanderers and Brahmans who haunt
the silent and remote recesses of
the forest say: when the body dissolves
after death they who break the precepts of
morality are reborn in the Waste,
the Woeful Way, the Fallen Place, the Pit.

Don't believe it. There is no other world,
no merit or demerit, no rebirth,
no karma. Nor is there heaven or hell
or fruit or result of deeds good or ill.

Trust only in things: hard things and soft things,
things that can be eaten and cannot,
fragrant things and things with an evil smell,
things movable and things immovable:
earth, trees, mountains and the lotus flower,
beasts, people and the music of the flute.

WINDOWS

If I had a window for every
dead plant I'd have a
balcony too,
jutting out like a statement of
fact and leaning on that balcony
            in springtime
a redhead in designer shades
            and nothing else
surveying with a smile
the dazzled traffic.

When workmen in yellow
jackets shelter from the
rain sharing cigarettes
a statue without a hand points to
the sky and the green lawn that would
            like to be
taller envies the ivy which
            curls and peeps in
at the cute redhead with
the stammer selling

couscous in the café
to a cus-cus-cus-
tomer. Where rooftops grow
green moss there is height and an ancient
tree shedding orange matter over
            everything.
The barber snips and trims and it
            is quiet in
this street, but last night a
window was broken.

Vesprajna

the consort of the god of water is sometimes shown pouring Him
    into different-shaped vessels
but is usually depicted drinking alone or feeding her four-headed
    cat who sits on the rooftops and stares at the moon.

Shakada

is often shown shopping or wandering through a shopping arcade
    enhaloed in black flames of longing and dread.
Half her body is living human flesh but the rest is decayed and
    swollen like dead livestock floating down the Ganges.
In her six hands she holds a cellphone, a cellphone, a cellphone, a
    cellphone, a cellphone, a cellphone, and she talks all night
    and all day.

Smä (or Enko)

is often depicted as a coil of wire or a magnetic field exerting
    a force on others.
He is generally (but not invariably) EVIL and is associated with
    leukaemia and other haematological neoplasms.

Psha

is represented in ancient paintings with his sacred animals the
    mongoose and the cobra
(the mongoose hates the cobra and the cobra hates the
    mongoose so they get into all kinds of madcap capers).
He is frequently depicted upright in an electric chair saying a
    prayer while the hair on his head and legs is shaved
by four muscular sailors, or sitting alone on a rented sofa in a
    Manhattan apartment quietly masturbating.

The ancient legends make much of his appetite for pornography
        and every new moon offerings of old copies of *Playboy* are left
in his tomb, but in midsummer he departs for the Underworld
        where his heart is divided into five pieces and consumed by
        five unforgiving females.

The Denades

are the ruthless invisible forces of Capital, spirits of profit and
        wealth and market domination.
They live abroad for tax purposes, but at summer solstice they
        return to influence the economy,
symbolised by the appearance of cardboard cities under
        freeways and lunatics ranting in public parks.

CODA

The God of Travel Flies First Class

The travel god travels home again, to eat and sleep
and fuck and found a future he has cursed,
flying over the heads of his children.
The first child coughs up curses, the second
nurses a bruise inside the shape of her father.

AFTER BIRTH

After birth.
After all this flesh
power of action
poem of the flesh: farewell!

Junkyard bones some corpses some
images of corpses some
old documentary
looking at corpses big corpses
little corpses corpses in the field
corpses in the street.

Can't remember
words. Can't walk
in the garden. Can't smell
the roses. Can't drink
a glass of water. Small
corpse on the water
floating
drifting
back to before
birth. Before all this
flesh, power of action,
poem of the flesh. Farewell!

BIG BUMPERTON ON THE SABBATH

after Johann Knopf (1866–1910)

'We are not concerned,' he said, 'with long-winded creations, with long-term beings. Our creatures will not be heroes of romances in many volumes.'
BRUNO SCHULZ, THE STREET OF CROCODILES

Love laughs at locksmiths.
HARRY HOUDINI

I

In a Christian house
In a Christian town
Lived a Christian man
With a little dog
That greeted him every day after work.

If Big Bumperton
(For that was his name)
Seemed a happy man
Then it only seemed
For he was alone since his mother died.

& in love, it's true,
He had little luck
For the girls he loved
Never did love him
& saw him as an object of pity.

Still he carried on
Hoping that the girl
Of his fevered dreams
Might one day appear
& love him & kiss him with her cherry-red lips.

But until that time
He would persevere,
For he had a shop
& his mongrel dog
To keep him company on winter nights.

Sitting by the fire
In his night attire
Bumperton was sure
That the Lord was there
Somewhere, glowing in the embers.

Gloomy solitude
With a mongrel dog
Sleeping on his lap,
So he spent his nights
& by day he was a locksmith.

& he had knowledge
Of every kind of lock,
Deadlock & padlock
& mortice & bolt,
But he lacked the key to a woman's heart.

Now our time is up.
Put another coin
In the poet's cap
& he'll tell you all
About Big Bumperton on the Sabbath.

II

On that Sabbath day
Bumperton was out
On his bicycle
Riding through the town
Doffing his hat to all the lovely ladies.

& he wobbled past
A poster on the wall
Of high-kicking chorus girls
With cherry-red lips
& endless layers of petticoats.

& he cycled on
Past a frozen lake
& a one-armed man
With a twisted mouth
Hurling pumpernickel across the sullen ice

(Which the geese ignored,
Having all flown south)
& a gaggle of girls
Skating on thin ice.
'What if one fell through?' he thought. 'Would I help?'

& he cycled on
Up a winding path
& the path was steep
But he peddled fast
& arrived at the snowy summit of a hill

Where he could look down
On the little town
& the chimney smoke
Curling to the sky
& Big Bumperton saw that it was good.

So he cycled on
Past the ruined house
Where an ancient crone
Cursed her final days
Before she was cast down the witches' tower.

Pausing by a sign
For another town
He took out his watch
& wrote down the time
In a pocket book, for he always liked to know

When he reached this point
In his weekly ride
On that holy day
When our Lord rested,
Before cycling home again for lunch.

& he pedalled on
Coming to a place
Where he hit a root
Hidden in the snow
& went flying over the handlebars.

III

Opening his eyes
After travelling
Far into his mind
For what seemed like days
(But was only a matter of minutes)

There in front of him,
Leaning over him,
In a milk-white dress
& with golden plaits
Was a girl with cherry-red lips.

'Fair queen of my heart,'
Sighed Big Bumperton.
'What was that?' she said.
'Please don't try to move,
You might have broken something in the fall.'

& with expert hands
She inspected him
For suspected breaks
In his arms & legs,
But Big Bumperton bore his pain within.

Then she sat him up
Lying in her lap
& she stroked his brow
& he bit his lip,
Fearing she might disappear if he spoke.

Gretchen was her name
& within a year
She became his wife
& he sold his dog
To the one-armed man, never shedding a tear.

Gretchen swept the house
& she filled the pot
With good things to eat
& he swelled with pride
That she had consented to be his bride.

IV

On the Sabbath day
Bumperton was out
On his bicycle
& he cycled deep
Into a forest where the birds around him sang cheep-cheep.

& anon a bird
Flew out of a tree
Making merry noise
Joyful melody
& each pleasant note became a word:

Sometime were we blessed,
Angels heavenly,
But our Master fell
For his wicked pride
& we fell with him for our offence.

But our trespass small,
God was merciful
& out of all pain
Set us here to sing
& to serve Him again, after His pleasing.

Down upon his knees
Fell Big Bumperton
& the bird said this
To him in that place,
Even as Big Bumperton trembled there:

Now have twelve months passed
That you have been wed,
But you still have not
Taken your delight
In the marriage bed, though it be your right.

In the second year
You shall see the place
That you so desire
Come to be usurped
& you shall enter the land of Bedlam.

Holy lightning struck
In his mortal brain
& the hills around
Cried aloud in pain
& holy storm clouds gathered, bringing rain.

V

Voices in the dark
Pleading to be free.
One of them is low,
One of them is shrill –
Big Bumperton is talking to himself.

'Hungry will I be
& cold showers take –
Holy punishment!
Punishment divine!
Spare me no humiliation!

O Lord, forgive them all,
These your ministers,
Of your purpose high
Ignorant entire.
I am punished for their disbelief.

Wisely did you send
Her into my bed
That my senses rent,
For without her sin
I would not have known innocence divine!

Divine innocence!
& I'll keep thy laws
Hallow thy Sabbath
Walk in the spirit
& make a new Heaven & a new Earth!'

VI

Big Bumperton is charged with electricity
Like a landscape
An abstraction
A magnified pupil.

After the electroshocks
He no longer understands locks
Or answers to his name or remembers
His late wife.

'Gentlemen, by means of this X-ray you can see
The patient has swallowed his front-door key
& a small pocket knife
With which he did the wicked deed.'

O Big Bumperton! Let others hurl insults – 'Madman!' 'Murderer!' –
While you ascend on your invisible bicycle
Ever closer to the cherry-red lips of your star,
A bright smiling star like a chorus girl.

ASHES

are bodies in disguise
mixing sighs and
tears in a lost garden.

An air of importance
permeates these
cosmonauts of
compost,

which the pomp of sky and stars
ignores.

Foolish men
inhabit their bodies like
metaphors.

DEATH OF A SENATOR

From whorehouse to hospital morgue
    They carried his bier
And questions were asked in the Senate
    Of an old bawd.

They carried his bier
    Talking of plans for a statue
Of an old bawd
    Following his coffin.

Talking of plans for a statue
    On the Statehouse lawn
Following his coffin
    From funeral to family plot.

On the Statehouse lawn
    His widow was led
From funeral to family plot
    To waltz with a mystery man.

His widow was led
    From palm lounge to dance floor
To waltz with a mystery man
    Suffused with exotic suspense.

From palm lounge to dance floor
    From war zone to uninhabited citadel
Suffused with exotic suspense
    Watched by the patient sniper.

From war zone to uninhabited citadel
    Her son ran in terror
Watched by the patient sniper
    Surrounded by drifting sands.

Her son ran in terror
    From whorehouse to hospital morgue
Surrounded by drifting sands
    And questions were asked in the Senate.

BIRDS

i.m. Anna Politkovskaya (1958–2006)

> *Your name is a – bird in my hand.*
> TSVETAEVA

They are shooting birds in Russia
to prevent the spread of

infection. The State Hygiene
Agency's instructions are

to shoot birds
in population centres

and in their nesting places.
'The shooting of birds is

pointless,' said one expert.
'Birds are very mobile

and there are so many
you can never exterminate

them all even if you give
every idiot a gun.'

ILLUSTRATED EVENINGS

Evenings were longer then, a winter chill
turned in the headlamps of returning care.

Street lighting and a confounding moon make pale
the carried and reluctant carrier.

Words sink like stones in the air.

So the weather drops another degree.
Pestered by their bodies, woken from dreams,
impatient invalids stoke the fire.

Something like this illustrated evenings ignore.
Difficult breathing, the worry of drums
and that season's native mystery.

PARASITE

. . . it did not want to love yet wanted to live on love.
THUS SPOKE ZARATHUSTRA

They breed on the branches of trees,
colonise the land, seek safety in numbers
and keep moist by drinking sugary soft drinks.

Vulnerable to the vagaries of the global economy,
they come upon white shores, ignorant of the inhabitants,
utter brief words, build bridges and sing of ages past.

Their children are small and brown well into adulthood,
when they are bought and sold, dropped from great heights
into enemy territory to become

bleached bones and souvenirs, perhaps
a television documentary, if they are lucky.
The unlucky are soon forgotten.

. . .

After a decade of treading water
he recalls his optimistic youth,
broods on abandoned loves, lost friends, dead-end jobs . . .

A line of boulders at the front door cannot be shifted.
He must find a new home, dashes out on to the moors,
follows predators and slams doors.

At midnight he sings the blues.
He is continually searching for her on long journeys.
She haunts him everywhere and communicates by shrill,
high-pitched shrieks.

JOAN MIRÓ
MAN AND WOMAN IN FRONT OF A PILE OF EXCREMENT

A turd like a curious
cobra or pagan idol, inwardly

trembling, knows this man and woman
of old. It is watching and waiting to see

if they are going to worship it or
destroy it. It would like to assume an air of

insouciance. *We should worship it,*
she says. *Worship a turd?*

Preposterous! says he, waving a tiny
pick-axe hand, his red snake fixing

its one eye on her fingers, aching to be
stroked and choked but

she is too busy holding up the sky.

IT TAKES A MAN

It takes a man in all he might be
heavy twisted rope of consequence
of no consequence
weighed in the balance and found wanting.
Not a man but a twister.

Outside the mob demanding: 'Who comes?
Who is it now dares speak for us,
for our lives?'

        The virtues work
        through us. They do not
        indwell. They do not
        inhere. They are not
        in here. There are no
        virtuous people
        only good acts,
        always virtue and its opposite –
        the virtues working through us.

It takes a man to unmake
his masculinity, to unmake
the man they made him.

We are come to this. Coming
here in all innocence, willing to hear,
willing to be made and unmade
and taught the virtue of checking
our facts, consistency, avoidance of error,
making a life appear reliable,
a narrative, a story we tell others:

        My name is . . . I live at . . . I am . . .
        I have . . . I want to . . . with you

that they may understand who it is
speaks to them today,

and who they are every day of their lives
until there are no more days.

Someone will come after me and say:
'This poem was said once, as I am saying it
now,
as others will say of me:

"He breathed – he spoke – he stood
in the garden at midnight and wondered
at the wonder of a mortal brain
coming to consciousness, the cruelty of a mortal brain
      coming to consciousness,
      the birth and death
      of individual consciousness."'

Living appeals, as you appeal
      to me, as I appeal to the gods – those crazy imaginary gods –
as I appeal to the soldiers
beating on my door

The great Emathian conqueror did spare
The house of Pindarus . . .

But in wartime
Husbands dragged from wives
Sons from mothers.

      At Rodez once
      the Nazis in retreat
      shot thirty maquisards,
      smashed in their skulls with stones
      to finish it. At Rodez in August 1944
      the day before the town was liberated.

At Rodez, the wind out of Rodez,
whipping the hill, whipping the old asylum
carrying the cries of the mad
to the townsfolk, the benighted townsfolk,
the cries of Antonin Artaud,
still awaiting liberation
at the psychiatric hospital
with its garden and little chapel,
the asylum where he grew his hair
and was visited nightly there
by his daughters of the heart.

EVERYBODY'S TALKING ABOUT ANTONIN ARTAUD

Everywhere I go
    People are talking about Antonin Artaud.

Turn on the radio
    Radio 2
        And it's *Pour en finir avec le jugement de dieu.*

Everywhere I go
    People are talking about Antonin Artaud.

Turn on the theatre of cruelty
    (I mean the TV)
        And the housemates are in the garden discussing Van Gogh,
            the man suicided by society.

And there's nothing the man in the street doesn't know
    About *Artaud le Momô*

Because everywhere I go
    People are talking about
        People are delirious about Antonin Artaud.

THE WASP AND THE ORCHID

. . . and your loves will be like the wasp and the orchid . . .
A THOUSAND PLATEAUS

Hiding its one
terrible testicle
underground it rises
Venus-like, immodest
bloom, complete with eyes,
antennae and wings,
its prominent labellum
('covered in long dense,
lustrous reddish hairs')
'similar in colour and structure
to the female wasp's
abdomen'. It even
smells the same: 'a floral
scent that imitates
the sex pheromone'.

Suckered by this
counterfeit come-on, it
attempts copulation
(properly 'pseudo-
copulation') – mounting
the labellum 'with
vigorous waving of
wings and abdominal
probing', 'the genital
claspers at the tip of
the abdomen partially
open'. The wasp becomes
a part of the orchid's
reproductive apparatus.
A becoming-wasp of the orchid.
A becoming-orchid of the wasp.

. . .

Having plucked
its rose it rests, horns of pollinia
on its head, before flying
on to the next false female.

ARMAGEDDON

The boy in the white nightgown
has escaped again. These woods

are damp. I am invisible.
Sincerely I believe in

the Society of Blood,
the Sick People and

the Mountain. I am still
listening to the sea,

still repeating myself. Something
has happened to my right hand.

It won't be polite to
the authorities, it won't

make a fist in the air.
Women always make

an impression. You
were tender beyond

compare. The memory
of the two of us does not

console. Your face, a
glowing coal.

I am weary of being
examined. I prophesy:

a wilderness is essential
to humankind, an indifferent

wildness, full of varied
shapes and colours, loves and

sympathies, and incapable
of guilt. Perhaps a violent

storm overnight could transform
this mute material,

shape it, as I never could.
Without the strictures of

a plot the results are
as we find them:

the crash of a statue
in the dark. I tried to

remember where I was going
and what it was you wanted

me to do. You always told me
I would die alone,

My Night Apple,
my little former friend.

BLACK JELLY BABY

*'. . . and there is no reason to demand
that immigrants should renounce
their nationalitarian belonging
or the cultural traits that cling
to their very being,'*
says Guattari in *The Three Ecologies*,
but don't try explaining this
to your friends down
the pub late one
evening after
work over
a few pints or
first the one will
denounce you:
      RACIST!
Then the other
(closer to your heart):
      RACIST!
white faces of anger and indignation.

Racist, they'll call you
racist and you'll try to
explain but they'll
call you racist
and storm out
into the night, and you'll sit
there many eyes upon
you and smoke another
cigarette with trembling
hand, then walk
home alone to your crappy
flat and wonder
what all that was about.

And the next day your
friends will send you
an email calling you
Enoch Powell
but lunchtime will bring
a bag of jelly babies by way of
a peace offering
and you'll take
one and one of them
will say: 'It's a black
one! It's a black one!'
and you're not sure if
you should eat a black
baby but you
eat it and they are
happy and you
chew the jelly baby
chew it all
up
and swallow it.

KISSING

On our last day
when I kissed you so
passionately, you had every right
to bite off my tongue and spit it out.

Instead you cried. I cried two
days later, listening to a Jew
on the radio describe
how he survived Auschwitz
by the skin of his teeth.

> The skin.
> The teeth.

DUST

For dust thou art, and unto dust shalt thou return.

GENESIS 3:19

Tout cela se résume finalement, pour reprendre Duchamp,
à un «élevage de poussière».

JEAN BAUDRILLARD

Dust over
everything. Nothing
but incomplete
exposures and
obscured views.

The ambiguity
of moving parts
never seen
in toto
and never explained.

Motionless pennants
and the heart
of a machine
beating, crystalline,
housed in an underwater
cavern, visited by
defeated characters
after dark
half-dressed and
curious, half-alive,
who die
if awoken,
before they can
touch
the beating heart that isn't a heart
but a natural formation in the rock
and there is no machine.

LOON
A STUDY IN HYGIENE

I

Lo!
Loon is
Loon was
alone and never alone
being in the world.

II

No!
Loon has
no past
no future
being in the present.

III

Loon forgets
everything. Also:
Loon forgets
everything.
(Memory is
unhygienic.)

IV

Loon has no
interior.
(This poem, too, is all
exterior.)

V

Loon was
Loon is
at the mercy of
encounters
events
sympathies
antipathies.

He flees
the sad
the anxious
neurotic
paranoid.

Sadness is
contagious.

A slave logic.

VI

Loon has experienced more than once a revelation, though seldom
any sense of levitation, being bound by the laws of gravitation, occa-
sioned by his inclination to inebriation, to which must also be
attributed his tendency to profanation and the occasional eructation,
through the incautious potation of liquids created by an ancient
process of fermentation and whose stimulation is generally held to
be the ruination of many a fine soul whose life ends in dissipation.
But far from making this a cause for lamentation, as would many
who find Loon a source of extreme irritation and look upon his irreg-
ular ambulation as a cause for disapprobation or even condemnation
or at the very least grounds for the confiscation, in accordance with
the relevant legislation, of what he fondly and without hesitation
calls his medication and only consolation, resulting in a confronta-
tion with those who would subject him to interrogation, using
insult and intimidation, with a view to his immediate transportation
or deportation, or who would at the very least, adopting a sombre

and serious intonation, call for his reformation, regarding him as a blight upon the nation, we offer no explanation, other than to point out the obvious correlation between Loon's desolation and his exaltation.

VII

Illness narrows Loon's
possibilities.
(Skip this part
if it tires you.)

VIII

Loon is
USELESS,
rejecting the capitalist values of production and exchange.

IX

In death did Loon transcend
in some inscrutable way
the matter of which he was composed?

X

He did not.

SILENT SPECTRES

*Last night I was in the Kingdom of Shadows. If you only knew how strange it is
to be there. It is a world without sound, without colour . . . It is not life but its
shadow, it is not motion but its soundless spectre.*
MAXIM GORKY ON FIRST SEEING A MOVING PICTURE

Sound is superfluous in
death's realm, in
faded prints.

Narrative lost, morbid
radiance,
shimmering

liquid tremor. They shudder
and blur, shift and
bulge as in

a funhouse mirror. Scuffed
snapshots of
reality passing,

most beautiful when
their strength is least
assured.

These shadows posturing
resemble dimly,
dimly recall

the duration of
bodies,
the ancient forms

empirical, action
reaction.
Is it still life

at 18 frames a second?
Is life only a question
of speed?

THE RAINY DAY MURDERS

Bring the girl into the basement,
The sophomore, and cast her down
On the bloodstained and mouldy mattress.
Let the Doberman Pinschers above bark
As you tie her to the wall, and let the wind
Through the broken window
Move the hooks descending,
Then everything goes into reverse and a happy ending.

Listen to her breathing,
Missing the people she trusts, the camper van
On the beach where she spent her last night,
The rain erasing all sign of a struggle.
If she has stopped hoping it is because
Your mouth is at her ear, so close
There can be no more pretending,
Then everything goes into reverse and a happy ending.

AN ACCIDENT IN SOHO

Your third marriage collapsed like an old barn.
The crash of it silenced the saloon-bar chatter

like the cry of a newborn.
You never expected to stumble and shatter

like a fumbled glass, or drown
among strangers in a bar.

On sunny days, the curtains drawn,
Pernod on tap but no beer,

the décor emerald green and gold,
your early promise unfulfilled,

you hid away from the world,
certain you had failed.

Your looks dropped away with the years
and the people you knew.

The son you stopped talking to cried real tears
at your funeral, but not for you.

LOST

lost in living

making love
and a little money

the heart
grieving

lost

attention
inattention
forgetting

the living connection
a habit
unromantic
unforgiving

INSOMNIA

She lies awake
if only to evoke
her body

in the dark

stretching
unveiling
her shoulders
like mountains
her pulsing heart

in the dark

an illustration
in a medieval
bestiary

ridiculous, too,
married to
a death to
come.

TIME REMAINING

I

I mature
like a rich quarter of town
with its own sense of
belonging –

not through propriety but
the passage of time –
enough days to make
a life, a clearing in
the forest.

II

Fields of grain
and a good life among
companions –

their grief a gathered
worship, the track of
a difficult birth –

open bones
troubled dust.

Some are carried
through a thousand
victories

others must lay down their lives
for a sigh.

Each has his goodness stolen.

III

My sight is
a standing flower

my sound
a rejoicing people

moderate in their convictions
and secure

in the growth
of their own minds

each restless but
awakened

and no one
taking offence.

IV

I like simplicity with
fortifications.

I am without
a language

lost in the fog of being
alive

of being a singular
thing.

V

I have been
robbed.

No doubt.

The law is
a mystery but
the ultimate paradox
must be a love without
bondage.

VI

It cannot be proved
but I discern a
sensation following
a sensation

like water in its
passing away

like waves towards
a better future

without prejudice without
collective hysterical
Humanity.

VII

Can you conceive
of a life where
everything is
a fragment and never
develops

exhausting
itself through
the distance it must travel
simply to be
a fragment?

VIII

All founded on
nothing, like you
said. Only your words
found it.

NOTES

CHAIN LETTER: 1 William Langland, *The Vision of Piers Plowman*; 2 John Gower, *Confessio Amantis*; 3 Geoffrey Chaucer, *The Canterbury Tales*; 4 Sir Thomas Wyatt, 'They fle from me that sometyme did me seke'; 5 Edmund Spenser, *The Faerie Queene*; 6 Sir Philip Sidney, *Astrophil and Stella*; 7 William Shakespeare, *A Midsummer Night's Dream*; 8 John Donne, 'The Broken Heart'; 9 John Milton, *Paradise Lost*; 10 Andrew Marvell, 'An Horation Ode upon Cromwel's Return from Ireland'; 11 John Dryden, 'The Hind and the Panther'; 12 Jonathan Swift, 'A Beautiful Young Nymph Going to Bed'; 13 Alexander Pope, 'An Epistle to Bathurst'; 14 Thomas Gray, 'Elegy Written in a Country Church Yard'; 15 Christopher Smart, 'Hymn II: Circumcision'; 16 William Blake, *Milton*; 17 Robert Burns, 'Tam o'Shanter'; 18 William Wordsworth, 'Old Man Travelling'; 19 Samuel Taylor Coleridge, 'Dejection. An Ode'; 20 George Gordon, Lord Byron, 'The Vision of Judgment'; 21 Percy Bysshe Shelley, 'The Sensitive-Plant'; 22 John Clare, 'I Am'; 23 John Keats, 'The Eve of St Agnes'; 24 Elizabeth Barrett Browning, 'Lord Walter's Wife'; 25 Alfred, Lord Tennyson, 'Ulysses'; 26 Robert Browning, 'My Last Duchess'; 27 Edward Lear, 'The Owl and the Pussy-Cat'; 28 Walt Whitman, *Leaves of Grass*; 29 Matthew Arnold, 'Dover Beach'; 30 Dante Gabriel Rossetti, 'Sudden Light'; 31 Christina Rossetti, 'The Thread of Life'; 32 Emily Dickinson, 'Safe in their alabaster chambers'; 33 Lewis Carroll, 'The Walrus and the Carpenter'; 34 Algernon Charles Swinburne, 'A Leave-taking'; 35 Thomas Hardy, 'After a Journey'; 36 Gerald Manley Hopkins, 'I wake and feel the fell of dark, not day'; 37 Oscar Wilde, *The Ballad of Reading Gaol*; 38 A.E. Housman, 'The laws of God, the laws of man'; 39 Rudyard Kipling, 'Mandalay'; 40 W. B. Yeats, 'Sailing to Byzantium'; 41 Gertrude Stein, *Stanzas in Meditation*; 42 Wallace Stevens 'Credences of Summer'; 43 James Joyce, 'The Ballad of Persse O'Reilly'; 44 William Carlos Williams, *Paterson* III; 45 Ezra Pound, Canto XXXIX; 46 D. H. Lawrence, 'The Mosquito'; 47 Siegfried Sassoon, 'Everyone Sang'; 48 Marianne Moore, 'The Mind is an Enchanting Thing'; 49 Rupert Brooke, 'The Soldier'; 50 T. S. Eliot, 'Lines to a Persian Cat'; 51 Wilfred Owen, 'Strange Meeting'; 52 e. e. cummings, 'Humanity i love you'; 53 Charles Reznikoff, *Jerusalem the Golden* (55); 54 Hart Crane, 'Powhatan's Daughter: The River'; 55 Laura Riding 'A City Seems'; 56 Langston Hughes, 'Cross'; 57 Stevie Smith, 'The Jungle Husband'; 58 Lorine Neidecker, 'Thomas Jefferson'; 59 Louis Zukofsky, *29 Poems* ('18'); 60 Kenneth Rexroth, 'Un Bel di Vedremo'; 61 Samuel Beckett, 'Ooftish'; 62 John Betjeman, 'In Westminster Abbey'; 63 W. H. Auden 'Taller to-day, we remember similar evenings'; 64 George Oppen, 'Party on Shipboard'; 65

Charles Olson, 'The Kingfishers'; 66 Elizabeth Bishop, 'The Fish'; 67 John Cage "25 Mesostics Re and Not Re Mark Tobey'; 68 R. S. Thomas, 'On the Farm'; 69 Dylan Thomas, 'Among Those Killed in the Dawn Raid was a Man Aged a Hundred'; 70 John Berryman, *Dream Songs* (47); 71 Robert Lowell, 'Skunk Hour'; 72 Lawrence Ferlinghetti, 'Autobiography'; 73 Robert Duncan, 'A Poem Beginning with a Line by Pindar'; 74 Barbara Guest, 'Twilight Polka Dots'; 75 Philip Larkin, 'Church Going'; 76 Jackson Mac Low, 'Trope Market'; 77 Philip Whalen, 'Sourdough Mountain Lookout'; 78 James Schuyler, 'The Crystal Lithium'; 79 Denise Levertov, 'Stepping Westward'; 80 Kenneth Koch, 'With Janice'; 81 Jack Spicer, 'Phonemics'; 82 Allen Ginsberg, 'This Form of Life Needs Sex'; 83 Frank O'Hara, 'The Day Lady Died'; 84 Paul Blackburn, 'The Once-over'; 85 Robert Creeley, 'The Door'; 86 John Ashbery, 'A Wave'; 87 Ed Dorn, *Gunslinger* II; 88 Thom Gunn, 'In Santa Maria del Popolo'; 89 Gregory Corso, 'Marriage'; 90 Gary Snyder, *Myths & Texts: Burning*; 91 Ted Hughes, 'A Childish Prank'; 92 Geoffrey Hill, 'An Apology for the Revival of Christian Architecture in England' ('The Laurel Axe'); 93 Sylvia Plath, 'Nick and the Candlestick'; 94 Diane di Prima, 'On Sitting Down to Write, I Decide Instead to Go to Fred Herko's Concert'; 95 Ted Berrigan, 'I Remember'; 96 Amiri Baraka, *AM/TRAK*; 97 Susan Howe, 'Speeches at the Barrier'; 98 Clark Coolidge, 'On Induction of the Hand'; 99 Seamus Heaney, 'Station Island'; 100 Lyn Hejinian, *My Life*; 101 Ron Padgett, 'Big Bluejay Composition'; 102 James Tate, 'Nausea, Coincidence'; 103 Alice Notley, 'Beginning with a Stain'; 104 Anne Waldman, 'skin Meat BONES (chant)'; 105 Bernadette Mayer, 'First turn to me . . . '; 106 Ron Silliman, *Paradise*; 107 David Shapiro, 'Dido to Aeneas'; 108 August Kleinzahler, 'A Case in Point'; 109 Charles Bernstein, 'The Klupzy Girl'; 110 Paul Muldoon, 'The More a Man Has the More a Man Wants'; 111 Maxine Chernoff, 'Breasts'.

CĀRVĀKA/LOKĀYATA: Lokayata was a materialistic system of Hindu philosophy that flourished around the first century CE. Its founder is said to have been Carvaka, whose dates are unknown. The writings of this school are no longer extant and all we know of it comes from the criticisms of its detractors. Cf. *Cārvāka/Lokāyata: An Anthology of Source Materials and Some Recent Studies*, ed. Debiprasad Chattopadhyaya (New Delhi: Indian Council of Philosophical Research, 1994).

BIG BUMPERTON ON THE SABBATH: The Outsider artist Johann Knopf was a locksmith who went insane and was diagnosed 'paranoid form of dementia praecox' (schizophrenia). One of his drawings is entitled *Big Bumperton on the Sabbath*. Knopf's illness emerged after the death of his mother, with whom he had lived, then a subsequent unhappy marriage. He suffered from religious delusions in which he believed he was a Christian martyr and could understand the language of birds, which he considered tragic creatures.

IT TAKES A MAN: *The great Emathian conqueror* . . . *Pindarus*: Cf. Milton's Sonnet VIII: 'When the assault was intended to the City'. Alexander's army sacked Thebes in 335 BCE, but he spared Pindar's house and showed mercy towards the late poet's descendents. *Rodez:* In 1937 the French poet and actor Antonin Artaud (1896–1948) was arrested in Dublin, repatriated and interned for nine years in a succession of psychiatric hospitals, including the asylum at Rodez in southern France. Here he created in his imagination the 'daughters of the heart to be born': feisty warrior-women bodyguards, based on ex-lovers (and two beloved grandmothers), who would protect him from the black magic of psychiatry.